MACDONALD STARTERS

Glass

Macdonald Educational

About Macdonald Starters

Macdonald Starters are vocabulary controlled information books for young children. More than ninety per cent of the words in the text will be in the reading vocabulary of the vast majority of young readers. Word and sentence length have also been carefully controlled.

Key new words associated with the topic of each book are repeated with picture explanations in the Starters dictionary at the end. The dictionary can also be used as an index for teaching children to look things up.

Teachers and experts have been consulted on the content and accuracy of the books.

Illustrated by: Ann and Michael Ricketts

Written and planned by: Diana Ferguson

Managing editor: Su Swallow

Production: Stephen Pawley, Vivienne Driscoll

Reading consultant: Donald Moyle, author of *The Teaching of Reading* and senior lecturer in education at Edge Hill College of Education

Chairman, teacher advisory panel: F. F. Blackwell, Director, Primary Extension Programme, National Council for Educational Technology; general inspector for schools (primary), London Borough of Croydon

Teacher panel: Loveday Harmer, Joy West, Enid Wilkinson

Series devised by: Peter Usborne

Colour reproduction by Colourcraftsmen Limited

© Macdonald and Company (Publishers) Limited 1974
ISBN 0 356 04630 3
Made and printed in Great Britain by Purnell & Sons Limited
Paulton, Somerset

Filmset by Layton-Sun Limited

First published 1974 by Macdonald and Company (Publishers) Limited
St. Giles House
49-50 Poland Street
London W1A 2LG

It is dinner-time.
I am drinking some orange juice
out of a glass.

1

Many things are made of glass.
Windows are made of glass.

2

Someone has broken this window.
The pieces of glass
are very sharp.

Mummy has poured boiling water
into a glass.
The glass has broken.

4

This car window is made
of special glass.
When the glass breaks
all the pieces stay together.

Here is a magnifying glass.
It makes things look bigger.

6

This man is wearing glasses.
They help him to see better.

Mirrors are made of glass.
Silver is put on the back
of the glass.
8

Here is a hall of mirrors.
These mirrors make you look funny.

9

glass

Glass is made from sand.
The sand is mixed with other things.
These are all melted together
in a furnace.
10

tube

The furnace is very hot.
The glass is soft when it comes out.
This man is blowing a bubble
in the glass.

11

Another man makes a jug
from the glass bubble.

This lady is making a glass animal.
She uses a very hot flame.
This makes the glass soft.

Sometimes people make patterns
in glass.
This wheel is for making patterns.
14

glass

These men are testing
some very strong glass.
The glass can hold up
three elephants.

15

People can make glass into strands.
The strands are called glass fibre.
Glass fibre is made in a furnace.
It comes out like this.

16

These men are making a part for a boat.
They mix glass fibre with resin.
They put it into a mould
to get hard.

This man is making
a stained glass window.
He cuts shapes from coloured glass.
He fixes the shapes together.

18

These stained glass windows
are very old.
They are in a big church in France.

19

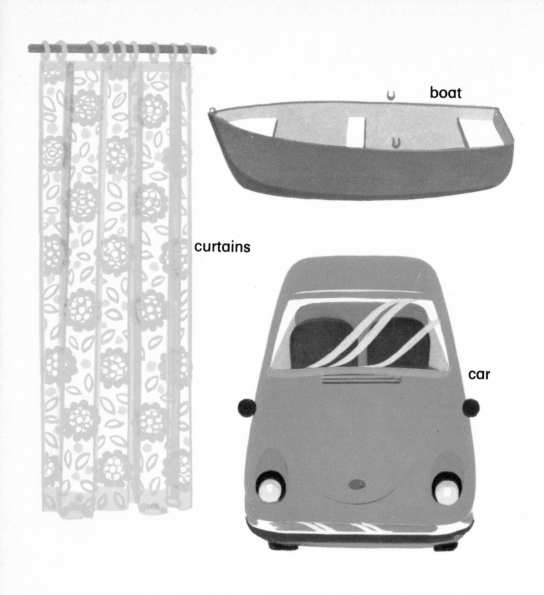

boat

curtains

car

Many things are made
from different kinds of glass.
20

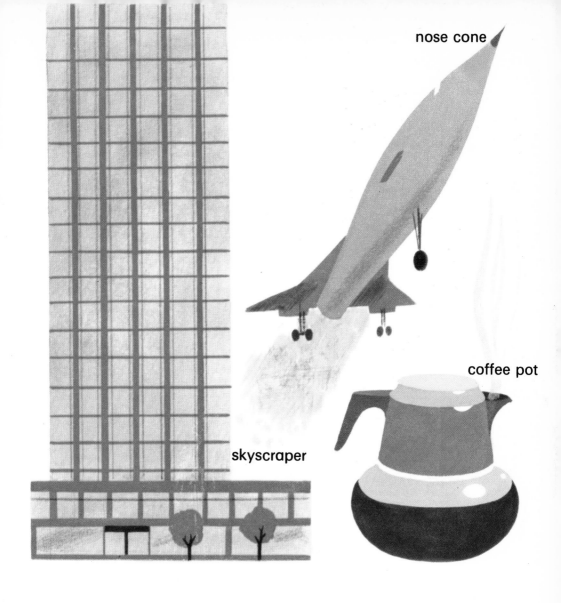

nose cone

coffee pot

skyscraper

Glass has been used
in all these things.

See for yourself
Make your own stained glass window.
Use black paper
and coloured cellophane.
22

Starter's **Glass** words

orange
juice
(page 1)

car
window
(page 5)

glass
(page 1)

magnifying
glass
(page 6)

window
(page 2)

glasses
(page 7)

pieces
(page 3)

mirror
(page 8)

23

hall of mirrors
(page 9)

sand
(page 10)

furnace
(page 10)

blow
(page 11)

bubble
(page 11)

tube
(page 11)

jug
(page 12)

animal
(page 13)

flame
(page 13)

patterns
(page 14)

24

wheel
(page 14)

boat
(page 20)

glass fibre
(page 16)

car
(page 20)

stained glass
(page 18)

skyscraper
(page 21)

church
(page 19)

coffee pot
(page 21)